D. U. M. P. IT!

DATING UNDER MY POTENTIAL

The Moore Family,

May God bless you
& prepare you towards
greatness! D.U.R.H.P.
anything that does not
propel you towards
greatness!
- Erika Moore

D. U. M. P. IT!

DATING UNDER MY POTENTIAL

Dr. Erika Lee

Ordering Information:

Orders by U.S. trade bookstores and wholesalers. Quantity sales. Special discounts are available on quantity purchases by corporations, associations, and others. For details, contact the publisher at the following email address:

Connect with Erika Lee:

Email:
Erikalee@pursefoundation.com

Instagram:
Instagram.com/purse_foundation_inc

Facebook:
Facebook.com/erikaleepursefoundation

ISBN: 978-0-578-95922-1

DEDICATION

To my mother, Ethel Lee, who taught me about God at an early age. I have a foundation I can always stand on, even when I fall. To my late father, Ezell Lee Jr., who taught me to stay in my lane, handle business first, and play later. To my adopted moms, Barbara Daniel & Mama Loni, who loved me like I was their own. Thank you for always encouraging and believing in me. To my siblings, nieces, nephews, cousins and god-children, take in the life lessons traveled by those before you and set out to blaze trails that will lead you to higher heights. To my friends who have always been there throughout the growth stages in my life, thank you for allowing me a place in your hearts. Lastly, thanks to all my exes for the experiences shared and life lessons learned. I am now better prepared to give and receive the love I deserve.

TABLE OF CONTENTS

Introduction 1

Shifted, Stretched & Shaped 3

Don't Delay Your Healing 31

Pretenders in Pursuit 37

Counterfeit Love 43

Intuition 49

Perfect Distraction 55

I Thought You Loved Me!!! 59

Holding on Too Tight 65

You're Moving Too Fast 69

Accepted to be Rejected 75

Keep Moving 79

D.U.M.P. IT 83

Sweet Reminders 87

About the Author 88

Introduction

This workbook is a culmination of relationship experiences presented in the form of art. It is designed to encourage group discussions and self-discovery through spiritual guidance. I'm not a relationship expert; however, I share my stunted and growth experiences with you to serve as a reminder to learn to be okay with letting go when a relationship no longer feels right or suits you. Our lives were not designed to take on people's problems and make them our own. We can have healthy and fulfilling dating relationships by first being healthy ourselves. In life, we are always learning, but that is not an excuse or reason to stay in the same seasons of life, taking the same classes and never passing the tests. The problem is not so much in making mistakes, but it is in not learning and continuously repeating them. The silly things you did in your twenties were called "age appropriate," but to still make those same mistakes in your fifties is what they call being an "old fool." Continue learning. Don't just live in a cycle of getting old and not growing.

·

Shifted, Stretched & Shaped

As a twenty year-old junior in college, I felt like I was sitting on top of the world. I had my own apartment, and my boyfriend known as Mr. Fly Guy. He was seven years my senior. The access he gave me to his car and home solidified my security in the relationship. He was from my hometown.We lived an hour away from each other, but the distance was never a problem. When we first met, I was still healing from a two-year relationship that had just ended. He was the perfect distraction that helped put an end to the hurt I was hiding on the inside. The relationship temporarily fed my quiet insecurities and unresolved pain. I would later learn we both had the same hidden agenda for connecting with each other. Within nine months of dating he proposed. It was my twenty-first birthday, and I did not see this coming at all. But I said "yes" and went to bed that night wondering how I was going to share the news with my mom. She didn't like him for me. Her reservations about him began two months after we started dating. I was home visiting from college, and he came by to take me out. She told me she was going to talk to him about rumors she had heard about him being married once he arrived. When he came inside, she looked him in the eye and said, "I want to ask you a question, and I want you to be honest with me, are you married?"

He answered my mother and said "no" with confidence. She said, "Okay. But if I find out you're lying, that's it!" My mom's "that's it" phrase meant she was through with you. And don't come this way again. Three months later, I received a phone call from a family member that sent shock waves through my body. I was informed my boyfriend was indeed married. I called him right away and asked him to tell me the truth. He constantly told me he was not married. Then he changed his story and said he had filed for divorce; technically, he was still married. He had deceived me, and it was easy to do. I was young, naïve, and lived in a different city. I was so angry that I immediately broke up with him.

We had been together for five months before I learned of his deceitfulness. The break up was tough on me; I missed him. After a month of not speaking, we eventually reconnected on the phone. He apologized for not being upfront and honest. He assured me that he cared and wanted a relationship. I wanted relief from the heartache, so I settled for a temporary solution. I chose to give in to my selfish desires and resumed dating him. Even when his divorce became final, my mother was still not happy. She believed he would always take more than he was willing and able to give. I had a way of always seeing the best in people, while overlooking their obvious flaws. This was truly one of my many downfalls.

When I graduated from college, I was offered a management position back in my hometown. It was a pivotal moment in my life. I was making close to fifty thousand dollars a year and living in a brand-new apartment. I found this position to be quite tough. I didn't have a lot of confidence and lacked experience in building relationships. I remember a conversation I had with my store manager. She told me I needed to shoot the breeze more and said I had an offbeat sense of humor. I was twenty-two and still learning myself and how to navigate my way around the workplace. I didn't like to engage in small talk. People getting too close to me made me afraid. I didn't want them to learn about my inadequacies. This job caused me a lot of stress. At the time, I was also pursuing my master's degree, in the process of purchasing my first home, and dealing with a fiancé who was no longer making any effort to meet my needs. I was trying to juggle it all, and I did for a while. But it came to an end like a domino effect. The first domino to go down was my relationship. We had been together for two years when I finally called it quits. The relationship had taken its course and hit a brick wall. It was time for both of us to officially move on. I was already living life as if I were single, and so was he. One Saturday morning, I got the confidence to close this chapter in my life. I drove to his house, and after he opened the door, I placed the ring in his hand. I thought about keeping the ring and possibly pawning it, but I needed to ensure he knew I was not holding on to him by keeping it. It hurt to let him go, but I had to keep pushing through the pain. It was time for me to stop living in darkness. I also still dealt with the guilt of dating him even after I found out he was married. I confessed my sins to God to become free from the burden that often convicted me and apologized to his ex-wife. Lastly, I had to forgive myself for the mistakes I made and vow to live a better life that was pleasing to God.

The next domino that fell apart in my life was having to walk away from my job. I had to make the decision to either leave my position willingly or be fired. I wasn't happy with my job, but I didn't want it to get to this point. I had always been the type of person to give my best to everything I did. I felt like a failure. My life was in a whirlwind of emotions, and things were steadily shifting. I had only been living in my recently purchased home for two months when I became house poor. I had no money to pay the mortgage or bills, but God sent angels who blessed me with the essentials I needed. After being out of work for months, I got a job working as a substitute teacher and mentor. I was able to gain my footing financially, and things were starting to look up for me. I obtained my master's degree, and after completing this milestone, I was ready for something new. It was finally time to relocate to another state. I had nothing holding me back; all I had to do was take a leap of faith. I didn't know where I wanted to move to, but I knew it was time. I wrote down several states I would consider moving to on strips of paper and placed them in a hat. I shook the hat up and then said a prayer. I asked God to allow me the chance to go to whichever state I pulled out. I put my hand in the hat, and I pulled out the state of Texas. At the time, I didn't know anyone who lived in Texas, so I wondered how I would even begin to embark upon this journey. A few days later, I was out walking my dog when my friend's step-father pulled his car over to the side of the street to ask me what I was doing with my life. I was happy to tell him that I was moving to Texas. He then asked me what part. I looked at him with a blatant stare. I didn't even think about or consider what city I would move to. All I knew was that I was moving to Texas.

Unsettled in my spirit, later that night, I decided to put the states in the hat again. This time, I pulled out the state of Georgia. I said a prayer about moving to this state, and all I can remember is the peace and calm I had about it. A few days later, I received a call from my friend asking if I would like to go to Georgia to celebrate his birthday. I was ecstatic! I felt like the hand of God was in my relocation plans. I had never been to Georgia and didn't know what to expect. While visiting, I was so smitten by all the greenery. I absolutely loved it and knew it was for me. When I returned home, I put my house on the market right away. It sold within two months, and I was ready to move with the money

I had profited from the sale. I booked a flight to Georgia to visit properties I saw online. I even had a plan to visit every company that required me to come in person to apply for a job. On a Wednesday in sweet November of 2007, I arrived in Georgia to put my search and plan into action. By Friday of that same week, I was offered two jobs and had secured an apartment. I knew relocating to Georgia was for me simply because God had provided the necessary resources for my survival. Within weeks, I was living in a new state. I was thankful for how everything worked out, but I learned pretty quickly that everything isn't all it appears to be. I had only been in my apartment for twelve days when my car was broken into. I couldn't believe someone would break into my car; it was an old Honda civic. I didn't tell my family about it because they would have told me to come back home. I decided to speak with the property manager about moving since I still had two days to cancel my lease. They moved me into one of their sister properties in another city. I felt much better about the surrounding area of this property. The apartment was even more updated than the one I was previously in.

I just had to get acclimated to my new job, which I loved. I had great hours and never had to pay for breakfast, lunch, or snacks because they were all part of the perks. On my first day of work, I walked into what was called the "console room" and remembered seeing the back of my male co-worker's head. He had nice waves with a fresh lining and voice of authority that commanded attention. He was handsome, and everyone seemed to like him. I liked him, too, but I wanted to keep my distance since we worked together; that would only last for so long.

After several months, we became a couple. Mr. Confidence swept me off my feet with his charm. I had never met someone who embodied so much confidence, and I was driven to him because of it. I just knew he was the one I was going to spend the rest of my life with. We had been together a little over a year when I decided to move in with him because I thought the move would bring us even closer. Slowly, the confident man I came to know turned into an angry, jealous man. He became angry if he saw me talking to my male co-workers and accused me of flirting with them. The accusations led to him placing me in choke holds and threatening to kill me. I never experienced a relationship that had me in fear of losing my life. I once lived in a blissful moment, dreaming about our future. But that was shattered by reality.

I stayed in the turbulent relationship, hoping for the return of the charming, caring person I first met, but things got worse. He had control over me that I could not explain; he had my mind. At work, I went out of my way to avoid conversations with male co-workers because I was scared of being accused of anything and dealing with the aftermath. I tried to prove daily that I was honest and that he could trust me. But this caused me to lose my identity. I relinquished control and submitted to a man I no longer knew. The following days were accompanied by emptiness and a dim light that no longer shined within me. I was being isolated and controlled. When I was at work and no one was around, I used the computer and googled the words "abusive relationships." While reading the articles, I realized I was being abused physically, emotionally, and mentally. I didn't want to be in a relationship with someone who had power over me. I knew the only one who could help was God. I started reading my word and praying daily for clarity. It didn't take long before God showed me the un-blinded truth about my life and relationship. The more I sought God, the more I was being empowered and reminded of how He wanted me to live an abundant life.

I made up my mind that I was going to get out of the relationship. I encouraged myself to leave, then reasoned on why I should stay. It took learning about my collegemate, Nova Henry, and her nine-month-old daughter, Ava, being fatally shot, to fully wake me up and get my attention. Their lives were taken at the hands of her ex-boyfriend. I knew what happened to Nova could very well happen to me because my partner carried a gun and often threatened me with it. I thought about the passing of Nova so much that I began to have dreams about her. In one of my dreams, the word **P. U. R. S. E.** appeared in black bold letters with periods between each letter. I remember waking up and asking God what "P.U.R.S.E." meant. The same day that I had the dream, I came across an article featuring Nova's mother, Yolan Henry. She was holding a purse as a symbolic gesture and stated that she must now serve as a voice for her daughter and granddaughter, who were victims of domestic violence. I believe God in that very moment, gave me a mission and purpose to make P. U. R. S. E. a confirmed reality. Inspired by a dream I would venture to help people in abusive relationships. I kept the dream hidden in my spirit until I was able to give my full attention to it.

Before I left my mentally-enslaved-and-draining relationship behind for good, my partner and I had a huge blow up. I found out he had been cheating and told him I was done with the relationship. Trying to end and leave an abusive relationship is the most dangerous time for a victim. This confrontation led to him pointing a gun at the back of my head and pulling the trigger. All I could do was think about how Nova and her daughter lost their lives. I thought I was going to die that night. He pulled the trigger, but it turned out to only make a clicking sound. I knew I had another chance to beg for my life. I told him I was sorry and didn't mean what I said. As I was crying and even asking God to spare my life, the angels were encamped around me that night because God blocked what could have ended in a tragedy. The next day, I knew I had to make a move because this relationship was going to end with me losing my life. I called a long-time friend and shared with him what I had been through in my relationship. I told him not to tell anyone, but being a friend, he had to look past what I wanted and do what was best for me. He shared the news with my mom. My mom called me the same day and helped me put a plan of escape in place. I was happy when I reached out for help; my friends and family reached in with their love and support. Although I was able to get out of my partner's house safely, I still had to face him at work. After we broke up, he ended up becoming my supervisor. He took pride in his reputation on the job, so conflict between us never arose while at work. A month later, I received a call regarding a job offer with another company. This was just the break I needed, but I froze. I had become so comfortable living in fear that I was scared to jump at the opportunity. I told the lady I had to pray about accepting the position and would call her back. I hung up the phone and started reminding myself that I was loved; this is a blessing from God. I called the lady back within five minutes and told her I would accept the offer. Even in my moment of being stuck in complacency, God had a plan and a way of escape. I just had to say "yes!" The next three years would consist of me healing, re-building my self-esteem, and getting back to the real me. The real me smiled just because I was breathing, laughed at my own jokes, and danced even when no music was playing. Life was simple before I got into the complicated relationship with Mr. Confidence. To get back to my life of order and simplicity, I spent quality time with God every morning. I prayed, worshiped, and studied the Word before starting my day. I did not date or entertain any romantic relationships. I worked out and bought clothes; it felt really good to do this without needing approval.

I even participated in a print ad model competition. The day of the competition, I put on my best outfit, straightened my hair, and made sure to arrive early to the location. I stood in line for an hour and finally made it to the front. The cameraman asked me to smile and pose. I left the shoot and hoped I would get a callback. To my surprise, I received a call the very next day. I had been selected to move forward in the competition, but I had to get people to vote for me in order to win. The outpour of support I received from others was phenomenal and boosted my confidence even more. Needless to say, I was one of the winners. The company picked me up in a limousine, took me to a warehouse to do a photo shoot, and awarded me with clothes and cash. My picture was used in advertisements in stores, on city buses, and on trains. I truly embraced all the love and excitement in my life during this time. I was determined not to let anyone ever steal my smile and dim my light. Then, I met Mr. Charmer, who came along and uncovered every wound and scab I thought had healed. Mr. Charmer pursued me even when I showed a lack of interest. I was flattered by his many attempts to get my attention, but three years of being single and practicing celibacy had me guarded. I wanted to give love another shot, so I finally obliged his request and went on a date. He was such a gentleman; we had a great time. We started spending more time together. I fell for him, and the excitement he brought into my life. I had our life together all planned out in my mind, but it didn't take long for my bubble to burst. Out of nowhere, he stopped pouring into the relationship. The time we spent together was replaced with empty text messages that read "wyd," which is short for what you doing. I settled for Mr. Charmer's blocked communication just to get my needs met by being in his life. The relationship never produced anything but a great deal of hurt and tables that were turned when I started pursuing him. Valentine's Day was coming up, and

I knew this day would be the tell-all if I needed to move on or stay in the relationship. He came over and gifted me with a Nike workout outfit. I was thankful for the gift, but for our first valentine's day, I was expecting sentiments like a card or stuffed animal with the words "I love you." I yearned for affirmation and validation that he loved me. The longer I held on to the relationship, the more I lived in confusion and starved off the crumbs he gave to me. It took some time before I realized this relationship, or "fake-ship," was all an illusion.

Mr. Charmer pursued me wearing his best mask. Once he got my attention, the game of chase was over for him. I was no longer a challenge to be conquered; there was no more resistance. He had achieved what he set out to do. I allowed myself to be cheated. I internalized this relationship as being normal because he never put his hands on me or was ever verbally abusive. I still lived in insecurity and remained unaware of who I was and the power I possessed. I had to start weaning myself off this one-sided relationship. In letting go of Mr. Charmer, I was able to focus on myself. I was even promoted at work and under contract to purchase my second home. The more I invested in myself, the more his interest seemed to return. Our yo-yo cycle relationship soon came to an end after he ignored my phone calls of distress. One night, I came home really tired after attending an event. Around three o'clock that morning, my home security alarm was tripped. I woke up scared. I had recently seen on the news that a woman was murdered by burglars who broke into her home. The only weapon of defense I had was my American Bulldog named Sugar. I gave her the command to go check the doors. She went downstairs, then gave a mean and vicious bark. I figured the burglar may have run out. Sugar came back upstairs, but I was still shaken. I went into my closet, locked the door, and called

9-1-1. I simultaneously opened the window and put my leg out in case I had to jump. I called Mr. Charmer several times to come to my rescue, but he didn't answer the phone. The police arrived and did a thorough check of my property's interior and exterior. Eventually, I learned I hadn't shut the back door all the way, so the strong winter winds pushed it wide open. My mind was still racing, so I called my friend Mr. Image to come over. Mr. Image really liked me, but my heart and mind were with Mr. Charmer. We spent the morning talking and decided to go get breakfast. As we were sitting in the restaurant waiting on our food, I saw Mr. Charmer and a woman walk past the window. I was livid! I told Mr. Image I would return to the table shortly. I went to meet Mr. Charmer at the door. As I approached him, he had a look of shock upon his face. I asked him who he was with, and he said, without hesitation, that the woman was his girlfriend. My heart dropped completely. I then walked past him and introduced myself to her. She was pleasant and unbothered. As I walked away, emotions of hurt took over my body, and I tripped over my own foot. I was too embarrassed to look back, but I was sure they saw me almost fall. I returned to the table with my composure intact. I didn't make mention of the incident to my friend, especially because I knew he liked me. Mr. Charmer and his girlfriend left the restaurant minutes after our encounter.

It all made sense why he could never give me his time; he was playing me. The hurt was too much to bear, so I followed the cliché: to get over your ex is to move on with the next. I gave my full attention to my friend, Mr. Image. I never meant for our friendship to be more than what it was, but I didn't take time to resolve my previous hurt. In doing so, false emotions ignited the start of our relationship. I met him at church. Service had ended and I was preparing to leave. I heard someone call my name, so I turned around.

Mr. Image introduced himself and informed me that one of our mutual friends told him my name. He was polished and had a nice radio voice. He asked me out for coffee, but I told him dinner would be fine. He laughed, but I was serious. We talked daily on the phone, and I enjoyed the conversations. But I knew he was not the type of man I was interested in. He came on very strong. After two months of getting to know each other, he gifted me with a Michael Kors purse for Christmas. I was surprised because it was still early in our friendship. This friendly gesture did cause me to pay a little more attention to him. I was hesitant about keeping the gift because we weren't in a relationship.

I often told him to take things slower with me because he always communicated his desire for a relationship. My heart and mind weren't connecting to allow an intimate space for him. I kept him in the friend zone until I was given some advice by one of my mother's good friends. She was a widowed woman in her eighties with spunk and the energy of a twenty year old. She wanted to see me happy and have a chance at love. She grabbed a sheet of paper and pen from the counter, and we sat down at my kitchen table. She asked me questions to determine Mr. Image's pros and cons. I felt like I was starring in a Tyler Perry movie and being taught a life lesson by Cicely Tyson. When she finished asking me questions, she said this man is an A plus on paper. She encouraged me to give the relationship a try, so I did. After a year of dating, he proposed. And I said "yes." I thought if we had a long engagement, I would be better prepared for marriage. I never had an example of what marriage was supposed to look like. My parents divorced when I was nine months old. Marriage was never a goal of mine to ever rush or jump into. I was still learning about myself and how to voice what I needed. I said "yes" because he was a nice guy, who I believed would care for me. I just needed more time for myself, but he had trouble letting the relationship breathe.

Prior to getting engaged we had our own homes, but he wanted to stay at my house all the time. I often asked him to give me time alone to recharge, but this request was usually ignored. My mother came to visit for a month; it was her first time seeing my new home in person. He came over daily and stayed every night with us. Months later, my mom told me how disappointed she was about it. I allowed him to push past my boundaries, so I silently suffered from an overdose of relationship suffocation. I had forced emotions and misunderstandings about what my man of God should be like. The most important piece that our relationship lacked for me was chemistry. I loved him but not the way a soon-to-be wife should. He had prepared to make me his wife by helping to eliminate debt on my credit card and giving all his furniture away to move in with me. We had gone so far in our relationship, but my heart and mind were still having problems syncing. With both of our needs going unmet, the relationship started to deteriorate. We completely fell apart when I became my dad's caretaker. I can't remember where I was, but I remember what I heard. God whispered in my spirit and said, "Shift!" I was scared. I didn't know what it meant to shift. I was taking a small group class at my church called Master Life and asked the prayer warriors to pray for me. I felt like something was getting ready to change in my life.

Months later, I received a phone call that my dad wasn't doing well, so I needed to go home. He was previously diagnosed with chronic lymphocytic leukemia (CLL). When I made it to Illinois and laid eyes on my dad, he looked so weak. He couldn't take three steps without becoming out of breath. I took him to the hospital, and he was admitted for a week. I stayed with him every night, sleeping on a little couch next to his bed. He was miserable, and his health was going downhill. I always told him that I would move him in with me if he ever became too sick to care for himself. He always blew me off, but I asked him if he would move in with me this time. To my surprise, he agreed. He only had one request. As he lay in the hospital bed, he looked up at me and said, "Don't get me down there and mistreat me." The words he spoke pierced my heart. He was an independent man, so for him to allow anyone, including me, to care for him was huge. I knew I had to show him he could count on me and assure him that he was not a burden through my actions. After my dad was discharged from the hospital, I had to act fast before his fears made him change his mind about relocating. I had to find a doctor to care for him and meet with a realtor to sell his home. I wanted to do everything in my power to make sure I got my dad to Atlanta.

Two days after he was discharged, he was living with me in Georgia. I didn't know how everything was going to work out, but I knew everything would work itself out. I couldn't leave my dad where he was; he needed me and didn't know how much I needed him, too. I was being stretched. I worked a full-time job, was engaged and had become a caregiver. My fiancé watched me go to work, come home, and put in more work to be available for my dad. He saw the toll it took on me and never once did he step in to help minimize the stress. No, he just added to it. He was more concerned about the lack of time we spent with each other. I had no energy to give to my relationship; my father's care was more important to me. It was hard work being a caretaker, but it was the most rewarding position. I will forever cherish it. My dad coming to live with me was a blessing in disguise. It showed me the current state of my relationship and what I could expect in my future with my fiancé, especially when experiencing adversity. The support I needed wasn't there.

Most importantly, the love I knew he needed wasn't there either. I had to make a decision to not go another day living a lie. I was experiencing the pit of life-weighed and torn down with disappointment. The pit was also the place where my transition to being repositioned would take place.

While in the pit, I learned to change my way of thinking about situations I had no control over and be content in waiting patiently on God to deliver me from life's trials. My pastor always said, "If you praise, you get raised. If you complain, you remain!" I praised my way through my pain. I had spent a good amount of time in the pit. All the dirt that landed on me was buried under my feet and served as my stepping stone. I was learning to stand on hurt and defeat. The change only came when I stopped running, embraced my pit, and let God have His way. I was being reshaped. I was the woman who was scared to let my light shine in fear of what others might say. I was the woman who would dim my light so that others wouldn't feel threatened. I was the woman who couldn't say "NO" without worrying if I had disappointed someone. I am now the woman who still sighs at the thought of rejection but welcomes it if it comes. I am the woman who no longer gives energy to people who don't reciprocate it. I am the woman who has learned how to set boundaries to protect my peace. I am the woman who has been **shifted** for strength, **stretched** for durability, and **shaped** for greater. Not that I have everything together, but I have been placed in a position where God can continuously work on me. I have been *shifted*, *stretched* & *shaped* for His glory!!!

The Archetypes

THE NARCISSIST

"Fret not thyself because of evildoers, neither be thou envious against the workers of iniquity."
Psalm 37 KJV

The narcissist is not the one to play with because they will change your entire life. The confidence they exude has a way of igniting a fire within you. They are a master at making you feel safe and secure. After much time, it becomes unsafe being with them. They can be fun people who take risks and live on the wild side and make you feel like you're living your best life. Out of nowhere, the sun stops shining. And all you have are dark clouds and rain in your forecast. The narcissist changes up everything you thought you knew and loved about them. The once caring person now lacks empathy and has no regard for your feelings. It's like you have become their enemy. You hold on to the relationship, waiting for them to show you love like they used to.

News flash! The narcissist has many issues and has kept up the front long enough to get you where they want you. You learn quickly to walk on eggshells because they can go off like a ticking time bomb. You try to adjust to their inconsistent personality, but they have you whipped into shape to march to the beat of their drum. The narcissist makes you feel paralyzed, like there is no way to escape their poisonous love. The narcissist never really changes; they just put the same moves on their next victim. They get worse if they don't seek help for their internal issues. One day they will meet their match. Karma will be sure to return all the hurt they have issued out.

Characteristics of a Narcissist
Abusive · Controlling · Lacks Empathy

THE ENTITLED

*"Pride goeth before destruction, and an haughty
spirit before a fall."*
Proverbs 16:18 KJV

The entitled person wants what they want and will disregard your boundaries to get it. They set out to have their needs met at the expense of hurting others. They are super confident people who have a grand view of themselves and expect people to treat them like the royalty they believe they are. Entitled people are good at giving you attention that makes you feel like a star. They might even buy you unexpected gifts and give you access to things early in the relationship, but you should be careful because they expect you to keep up their status quo even when they stop pouring into the relationship by clinging to you for monetary resources.

They will switch up their moods on you like undergarments and think nothing of it. They get bored easily and always have someone waiting in the wings. Avoid being engulfed by their exterior and be in tune with the vibes and energy they give off to you and others. If they do more talking than listening to you, pay attention because their self-absorption and entitlement is at work. Entitled people can affect your spirit and mental health. Being with them feels like you've met the one, but they are just a temporary pit stop that comes with unnecessary heartache and wasted time.

Characteristics of the Entitled
Self-Absorbed · Arrogant · Egotistical

THE MANIPULATOR

"Woe unto them that call evil good, and good evil; that put darkness for light, and light for darkness; that put bitter for sweet, and sweet for bitter!"
Isaiah 5:20 KJV

The manipulator comes on strong and gives you a renewed excitement for life. They hide behind their many insecurities that are invisible to the naked eye and guarded heart. The manipulator is goal-oriented and sets out to accomplish what they want. They possess a mysteriousness that makes you excited to be around and learn everything about them. The manipulator knows what it takes to get your attention and win you over. Once they have worked their way into your heart, you start giving them the attention they were giving you. But they quickly lose interest. Manipulators are really insecure people who will leave you without warning.

They wear the best mask, but don't lose sight of yourself. If you begin to feel like you need to cook more, dress better, or buy them things to regain their attention, you are in their well-designed trap and have already started running on their hamster wheel. Remember, they love to conquer, not necessarily be conquered. Avoid their inconsistent patterns of love that leave you wondering when they will make quality time for you. If you have to ask for their time, just know you're not the only one on their mind.

Characteristics of a Manipulator
Deceitful · Schemer · Charmer

THE CONTROLLER

"Look not every man on his own things,
but every man also on the things of others."
Philippians 2-4 KJV

The controller comes across as very gentle in nature and reminds you that chivalry is not dead. They are all about looking the part rather than playing it. They will celebrate your wins and successes only if they shine light in their direction. The controller knows how to appear before people, showing their affection toward you in public and dismissing you in private. They are all about the show and love a good audience that watches while they perform. The controller makes you look like the most desired person on the planet in front of your friends and family. In return for making you look good, they demand your full attention and get jealous if your energy is given to anyone else. They have to be number one, or there will be hell on your hands. Their need for attention and affirmation will cost you all your time. Having your me time is rare and not long enough to recoup from the energy they drain you of.

The controller looks the part to everyone else, but you know the truth-the real person behind the scenes. They don't mind you being in the spotlight as long as it does not cost you being away from them. The controller can be detected by their child-like behavior of wanting you all to themselves. They portray the role of having it all together. They are experts at controlling the narrative and storyline.

Avoid being trapped in the world of the controller because they will have you starring in the role of the perfect puppet.

Characteristics of a Controller
Immature · Selfish · Jealous

Relationship
Experiences

Don't Delay Your Healing

*"Come unto me, all ye that labour and are heavy laden,
and I will give you rest. Take my yoke upon you,
and learn of me; for I am meek and lowly in heart:
and ye shall find rest unto your souls.
For my yoke is easy, and my burden is light."*
Matthew 11: 28-30 KJV

Kenny's Story

Delaying doing something in order to avoid present hurt or discomfort will not only delay what is already to come, but it will increase the pain you will feel in the future. When you purchase groceries, you will notice on the package that it may read "best if used by (or before)" a certain date. As people, we do not have a "best if used by" sign, label, or stamp on our bodies. But we know when something does not feel, look, or taste as it should. The same relates to relationships. I'm sure you remember when your partner was giving you their best; now, the word "best" seems no longer existent based on their actions. We have no problem protecting our bodies by getting rid of spoiled and expired food products; however, we hold on to being unhappy, emotionally unstable, and mentally drained. We endure yoyo mood swings and gather crumbs from an unhealthy relationship. If someone is not giving their best to you, know they cannot bring out the best in you!

If you **delay** getting rid of the expired baggage in your life, you will continue to live in **denial**, unwilling to change what is making you sick. Your **delay** and **denial** will cause **deferment** of better things to come because there is no room for the new, when the old still exists. Your continued journey through **destruction** will take away your **determination** to seek or think that you can **do** better. Only you truly know if you have expired contents in your life that need to be tossed out. Stop holding on to what is not holding on to you. Rid your life of false admirers, future fakers, joy killers, or anyone who does not bring out the best in you! Don't delay your healing! Get back to dreaming. Get back to happiness. Get back to laughing. Get back to smiling. Get back to believing. Get back to setting and achieving goals. Get back to YOU!!!

QUESTIONS FOR SELF-DISCOVERY

1. Kenny is delaying ending a relationship, what advice would you give him?

_____

_____

_____

2. What are some reasons people stay in relationships that no longer benefit them?

_____

_____

_____

3. How do you know when it's time to put closure to a relationship?

_____

_____

_____

Notes

_____

_____

_____

_____

_____

_____

_____

_____

_____

_____

_____

_____

_____

_____

_____

_____

_____

Notes

Pretenders in Pursuit

*"Above all else, guard your heart, for
everything you do flows from it."*
Proverbs 4:23 KJV

Toya's Story

Have you ever met a person who appeared to have it
all together? You got with them thinking, *Yes, finally
someone who has something to offer me*. They seemed like
they loved God. Heck, you even met them in church. They
had a good job, nice car, and their own place. Looking at the
exterior and material status of a person will surely set you
up for failure. As you engage in regular conversation or date
this person, they become relaxed. So comfortable, their real
self is unveiled. You realize they need you more than you
need them, especially financially. You become their standby
ATM, which simply means whatever money you have
becomes Automatically Their Money! Slowly, you're asked
for resources to help fund their trendy lifestyle while they
give you the minimum in everything else. They are actually
broke, but they try to keep something they never could
afford. Thank goodness they have you, right? No good! They
looked the part, but they were playing a shabby role!

So let's address the car they're driving. The BMW is nice
and all, but you realize it's all they have, especially when

they pull up to their apartment complex. Oh, the clothes they're wearing? They gained every piece from previous relationships. They're just waiting for you to pull out your credit card and contribute to their closet fund. These people can be referred to as **pretenders. Pretenders** are people who write fraudulent and post-dated checks to string you along for another week, month, or year until they use you up and move on. They make empty promises they never come through on. When you are finally ready to cash in on the relationship, you find out you were just a void they needed to fill in their life. You're now left in the negative, in the hole, without resources, and empty!!!

Mr. or Ms. Pretender don't only attack you financially, but they hurt you mentally and emotionally. They will steal your heart and tell you how they were done wrong in past relationships, hoping to gain your empathy. **Pretenders** do a good job of making you think they were only single because they could not find someone to treat them right or that they just hadn't met the right one. **Pretenders** come on strong; they pursue you hard. After a while, the tables become turned so that you begin pursuing them. You start doing all you can to make the relationship work. You put in overtime, trying to get your needs met like how they were in the beginning. You keep trying until you realize they got away with stealing your heart and gave it back to you broken! **Pretenders** are dangerous people who live double lives. They pretend because they know they are not worthy of you. To pretend, you have to know who you already are in order to act out a role that portrays someone more appealing.

Many of us have given our hearts to intangible things and people, exposing ourselves to unsafe, hazardous conditions. But guard your heart! It is valuable, comes from a special lot, and is the only one you got. It's way too delicate to let anyone handle it who does not plan to help safeguard it with you. So don't focus on the exterior only because it can cloud your vision, making you incapable of seeing a pretender in pursuit. **Pretenders** are people with words but no actions, leaving you to love their possible potential rather than their present reality! Beware of the pursuit and guard your heart!!!

QUESTIONS FOR SELF-DISCOVERY

1. When do you think Toya should have realized she was being pursued by a pretender?

_____

_____

_____

2. Have you ever had someone claim to be someone they were not? Explain.

_____

_____

_____

3. What can you learn from Toya's experience that you can possibly share with others to help them better recognize a pretender in pursuit?

_____

_____

_____

Notes

Notes

COUNTERFEIT LOVE

"But I trusted in thee, O LORD: I said, Thou art my God. My times are in thy hand: deliver me from the hand of mine enemies, and from them that persecute me."
Psalm 31:14-15 KJV

Sharon's Story

I have been sick for a while and didn't even know it. I had been dying for years from the well-known disease called **LOVE**. My doctor informed me that, although love is good and we all need it flowing through us, there are counterfeit forms that are bad for my health. He told me that I had one of the worst counterfeits of love lurking in my body. The love in me started out pure but had been contaminated by receiving from someone what I thought was the right kind of love; it was the wrong kind of love. I had been infected by someone who had the selfish love disease. You're familiar with this disease, right? The selfish love disease is a counterfeit of selfless love. This disease causes you to give your time, energy, efforts, love, mind, and heart. And in return, you receive little or nothing in order to be replenished of the things you have given. The doctor asked me if I had experienced any of the following symptoms: feeling overwhelmed, like I have given my all with no more to give; forgetting about my own needs; or being a people-pleaser.

The doctor asked if I was codependent, a slave to a fool, or submissive while experiencing dismissive attitudes. Doctor, oh doctor, I have had all of these symptoms for years, and I thought this was normal because I had been operating in them for so long. I did not realize this wrong love had kept me from pursuing my purpose, dreams, and goals. This selfish love I was receiving only allowed me to focus on the pain I was enduring. The doctor told me that if I continued to allow the wrong love to attach itself to me, I would die slowly of mental anguish, anxiety, and depression. I'm glad he told me I was not at the final stage of needing a heart transplant. The test results confirmed I am still able to give and receive love.

Although I have been slowly dying, the doctor said my heart problems could be rectified. Yes, a cure! He said the procedure would not cost any money. Yes, the cure is free! He told me all I had to do was go and seek the head doctor because he had all the answers to every question, thought, or worry anyone may have.

I asked, "Doctor, can I have the name and address of this head doctor who can cure me?"

"Sure. His name is Jesus, and His address is wherever you are."

The doctor told me Jesus is everywhere, and he wanted me to find a secret place where I could get alone and talk to Him without any distractions. The doctor told me Jesus would heal my body, regulate my thoughts, and renew my mind and spirit. I just had to be ready and willing to deny myself, take up my cross, and follow Jesus from this day forward.

Doctor, I want to know how it feels to have joy. I have to know how it feels to have peace of mind and experience unconditional love. Thank you, doctor! I am going to go get my healing. As I made it home, I made my way to the closet, fell to my knees, and asked Jesus to take the selfish love disease I had been infected with away. I no longer wanted to continue pleasing others, especially in ways that were not pleasing to Him. I've allowed man to take His place. I asked Jesus to remove anyone and anything that had been hindering me in my spirit. I realized I could not do anything apart from Him, so I asked Him to please forgive and restore me. We all desire to be loved, but we must be careful of counterfeit love. You'll know it when you feel it; it asks for much of you and gives you little in return!

QUESTIONS FOR SELF-DISCOVERY

1. What advice would you give Sharon or someone if they feel like they are giving more to the relationship than their partner?

_____

_____

_____

2. What self-care practice would you perform for yourself after being misused?

_____

_____

_____

3. How can you identify when the love being shown and or given to you is harmful to your overall well-being?

_____

_____

_____

Notes

_____

_____

_____

_____

_____

_____

_____

_____

_____

_____

_____

_____

_____

_____

_____

_____

Notes

INTUITION

"Trust in the LORD with all thine heart; and lean not unto thine own understanding.   In all thy ways acknowledge him, and he shall direct thy paths."
Proverbs 3:5-6 KJV

Keisha's Story

I carried you for more than nine months. I didn't have morning sickness or any food cravings. I gained so much weight and couldn't wait for my due date. Trying to embrace my new normal, all I could do was pray and hope for a successful delivery. To my surprise, my delivery took years. I was pregnant with anxiety, fear, rejection, and doubt. I had to learn how to rid myself of these insecurities that went against everything that could produce healthiness within me. Being impregnated with insecurities had me calling negative things positive and positive things negative. I was tired of carrying the burdensome load that was weighing me down. I was weighed down by unfulfilled expectations along with his raised hands that came against me. He expressed threats from his tongue to my ears, heart, and soul. I didn't want to believe I was in another bad relationship. It was time for me to stop suffocating the gift of intuition that was inside me. Without intuition, I lived in denial, not wanting to see or know the truth. The more I leaned into my intuition, the contractions became greater and more frequent. Insecurities and intuition just did not mix.

My insecurities kept me held in bondage while intuition freed me from the blinders, gave me immediate understanding, and allowed me to know something was not right. It was time for me to deliver. Instead of delivering, I was delivered from the evil roots that tried to kill purpose and promise, drive out light to block love, and keep hurt from healing, vision from victory, and rest from replenishing. Intuition has given full birth. I now listen ever so carefully to the still small voice in every season as I am reminded the gift of intuition is inside me for a reason.

QUESTIONS FOR SELF-DISCOVERY

1. What advice would you give Keisha or someone who has found themselves in another bad relationship with a different person?

_____

_____

_____

2. What behavioral patterns have you contributed that allowed your current relationship to mirror your past relationships?

_____

_____

_____

3. What steps will you implement to check in on yourself to ensure you don't ignore your intuition?

_____

_____

_____

Notes

Notes

PERFECT DISTRACTION

"Set your affection on things above,
not on things on the earth."
Colossians 3:2 KJV

James' Story

I was healing from a past unfulfilled relationship that had broken me. I thought the pain would last forever, but the perfect distraction came. My pain temporarily went away. I was in the stage of needing to keep my bandages on, but I chose to expose my wounds and entrust another with my care. I wanted love but neglected the prerequisites of healing and taking my time. I entered love blindly, not even wanting to see the truth. My perfect distraction had unresolved issues and also needed healing. How can two sick people care for each other without becoming sicker? We were two empty glasses trying to pour into each other. I wanted what I envisioned for my life, so I forced feelings, energy, and love to fit into my view. My view shattered into pieces that mirrored what I was feeling on the inside. I was broken, running to anyone with skills of repair. I wanted change, but I continued with my old patterns of love and was shortchanged of what I desired. My eyes are now open; my heart is guarded. I'm getting better now that my perfect distraction has departed.

QUESTIONS FOR SELF-DISCOVERY

1. How could James have avoided encountering more pain in his new relationship?

_____

_____

_____

2. Have you taken time to heal from your past relationship prior to entering into a new one?

_____

_____

_____

3. How would you handle being in a relationship only to discover your partner is not exactly in an emotional state to be with you?

_____

_____

_____

Notes

Notes

I Thought You Loved Me!!!

"He heals the brokenhearted and binds up their wounds."
Psalms 147:3 KJV

Nicole's Story

Have you ever been a victim of someone who was just in love with the *chase*? They did all the right things while pursuing you, but once they got you, they became completely clueless on how to keep you! They loved the challenge you provided. Subconsciously, they were trying to prove you were not who you claimed to be just because they lacked integrity. Once a chaser has worked their charm on you and made you feel comfortable enough to let down your guard, they begin to slowly withdraw from you. You begin to ask yourself, What the heck am I doing wrong? Don't internalize their actions by blaming yourself. Oftentimes, they are emotionally unavailable. They realized they could no longer put up a front because things progressed in the relationship. It got to a point where they would have to deliver on those fake promises they made.

The chaser is a part of the **C-Family**; their first cousins are the **U-Family.** Both families are good at making you believe you have found a godsend! Let's take a look at some of the **C and U-Family** members. In the C-Family, you have cousins Conniving, Control, Careless, and Charmer. The **C-Family** thinks they are better than their cousins in the **U-Family.** I'm not sure why because they are all so much alike. The **U-Family** consists of Uncommitted, Unreliable, Untruthful, and Unavailable. Stay away from the **C** and **U-Family** members if you can. Remember, your relationship with these family members is no exception to the rule. They may have different routes and routines, but quite often they will take you to the same destination—**heartbreak**!

God wants you to be happy. Anything or anyone who constantly drains, depletes, or diminishes your character is not who God has intended for you to be with. They may have pursued you well and lost interest once you reciprocated. This simply means you need to opt out of allowing your mind to be tangled and rattled with such confusion. Wherever there is confusion and the absence of clarity, you can be sure that some form of abuse will follow. If you have already encountered these family members, know that you are not alone. Continue to love yourself through the pain and smile through the hurt. Life may not be all peaches and roses, but surely the love that's for you will one day emerge.

QUESTIONS FOR SELF-DISCOVERY

1. What advice would you have given to Nicole when she noticed inconsistency during the courtship stage?

_____

_____

_____

2. Have you ever been pursued by someone, and they stopped chasing you once you showed interest?

_____

_____

_____

3. What did you do to try to regain their attention?

_____

_____

_____

Notes

Notes

Holding on Too Tight

"For I know the thoughts that I think toward you, saith the LORD, thoughts of peace, and not of evil, to give you an expected end."
Jeremiah 29:1 KJV

Melissa's Story

I didn't know love was supposed to inhale and exhale my air! Almost incapable of doing things on my own. I feel disabled when you're not around because of the dysfunction that has been going on for so long. I can't make up my mind without you. I don't even know what I want to eat if I'm not eating with you. I allowed you to hold me too tight and cut off my air supply. Now my brain relies on you to think for me. You're holding me too tight! Inserting yourself in positions you're not supposed to occupy. No longer do you spy or need to. You have access to everything, including the inner me and even the worst of me. Who am I? I've lost control over my wants, desires, and thoughts. You're holding me too tight! There is no more vision or clarity. No sound voice of reasoning. Just a mouth that won't open and a heart that is frozen. I can't breathe because you're suffocating me!

QUESTIONS FOR SELF-DISCOVERY

1. How would you advise Melissa to communicate her need for space to her partner?

_____

_____

_____

2. Have you ever felt like you were not getting the time alone you needed for yourself in a relationship?

_____

_____

_____

3. Have you ever lost yourself in a relationship because you were doing what someone else wanted you to do?

_____

_____

_____

Notes

Notes

You're Moving Too Fast

"But they that wait upon the LORD shall renew their strength; they shall mount up with wings as eagles; they shall run, and not be weary; and they shall walk, and not faint."
Isaiah 40:31 KJV

Brian's Story

It used to beat at a calm pace, now it beats with palpitations. Working it too hard can cause tiredness and weariness. My heart can only beat so fast. If you tried to make it match your rhythm, it probably would go into cardiac arrest. My mind wants to do certain things with you, but my heart won't connect. I need time, space, gentleness, and a consistent pace. We both have two different beats right now. I can't keep up with you because your endurance level often increases. You put pressure on me to take it up, but my heart can only beat so fast. When your expectations increase and mine stay the same, conflict arises that causes you to label me as selfish and controlling. These labels are not true. Your expectations are greater, which causes voids within you that are not being fulfilled by me. It may seem like it's controlling, but I'm just maintaining control of my heartbeat. I have tried to fill your voids by giving more just to keep you in the race. It's too much on my body right now.

My pace is slower, but I refuse to rush through levels that are necessary for building my endurance. I don't want to operate with a false start, but you're moving too fast for my heart!

QUESTIONS FOR SELF-DISCOVERY

1. How should Brian have handled his partner pushing past his boundaries?

_____

_____

_____

2. Have you ever had someone pressure you to do things before you were ready?

_____

_____

_____

3. Why do you think people move so fast when dating?

_____

_____

_____

Notes

Notes

ACCEPTED TO BE REJECTED

"The stone that the builders rejected has now become the cornerstone."
Psalm 118:22 KJV

Chloe's Story

I learned how to quiet my voice, take a back seat, and let the blind lead. You accept me for who you want me to be while rejecting the real me. Intimidated by my strength and motivation, you delight in my sad emotions. You don't realize your own capability and find it easy to dismiss rather than embrace me. I tried to master avoiding hurt and indirectly became a people pleaser. Overly pleasing with my words, actions, and giving. Dimming my light so that I wouldn't shine so bright. I gave in for my peace, but instead I was met with calamity. Like a puppet, you manipulate the strings attached and have me in line like a disciplined soldier. The inability to live freely is due to me accepting your deficiency. I have stunted my growth by tiptoeing through life afraid to live out loud. I wasn't born in a box and will not allow myself to be kept in one. Accepting all that encompasses me and rejecting the dysfunctions I learned to carry. My worth is not defined by acceptance. Experiencing your rejection has been the protection that has led me in a new direction.

QUESTIONS FOR SELF-DISCOVERY

1. How has pleasing people affected you within your relationships?

_____

_____

_____

2. Why do you feel the need to please others?

_____

_____

_____

3. What are some words of affirmation you can say to remind yourself to avoid pleasing people?

_____

_____

_____

Notes

Notes

KEEP MOVING

"Brethren, I count not myself to have apprehended: but this one thing I do, forgetting those things which are behind, and reaching forth unto those things which are before, [1]I press toward the mark for the prize of the high calling of God in Christ Jesus."
Philippians 3:13-14 KJV

Madison's Encouragement

Keep moving when life has you down

Keep moving when you want to smile but all you can do is sigh & frown

Keep moving when you want to throw in the towel

Keep moving when you want to stay but know you have to go anyway

Keep moving when you have been rejected & misunderstood

Keep moving when you have given your all & encountered many falls

Keep moving because you know greater is coming

Keep moving because you know a delay does not mean a denial

Keep moving because you know where your help comes from

Keep moving because you can look back & already see what He has brought you through!

Keep moving because you know that God is before you!!!

QUESTIONS FOR SELF-DISCOVERY

1. What was the toughest moment in your life that you thought would stop you from moving on but kept you going?

_____

_____

_____

2. What are some of the ways you moved on from difficult relationships?

_____

_____

_____

3. What has been the outcome of learning how to keep going in the face of adversity?

_____

_____

_____

Notes

_____

_____

_____

_____

_____

_____

_____

_____

_____

_____

_____

_____

_____

_____

_____

_____

_____

Notes

D.U.M.P. IT

"These things have I spoken unto you, that in me you might have peace. In the world you should have tribulation, but be of good cheer; I have already overcome the world."
John 16:33 KJV

Dating Under My Potential

I continually attracted partners who were hurting and hiding. Giving attention to their unspoken needs, I saw the best in them even when they didn't see it in themselves. My strengths of being a fixer, helper, and problem solver became my weaknesses. My boundaries seemed non-existent, so they didn't keep me from being misused or overly extending myself. Like a socket with no power, switch with no light, or television without a picture, I was overwhelmed while trying to make broken things work. Collecting the trash of unwarranted hurt and disappointment, I had become an invisible receptacle. I had to stop being the common denominator that determined the same factor of results. In order to go higher, life required me to work on myself. I carried a fragile heart. Dismissed red flags for the sake of just wanting to be happy. Stayed too long even when the warning signs became physical. Settling for less was no longer an option. I learned to embrace who I am. I let go of fears about being misunderstood and judged. I forgave myself and others. The more I invested in myself, the more fulfilling relationships I encountered.

One positive outcome from my failed relationships is that I always return back to my first love—God. His power released me from the strongholds the wrong love had over me. My Label Maker & Creator has plans to prosper me and not harm me. Plans to give me hope and a future. We are not called to live life without encountering disappointments just because we are believers, but God wants us to count it all joy when adversity comes our way. Learning how to bounce back from temporary knockouts is the very essence of life.

You may have heard the saying, "Show me who your friends are, and I'll tell you who you are!" I believe the relationships we choose with others mirrors our reflection of where we are mentally, emotionally, and spiritually. Working to be stronger and better in the areas of self-care and self-worth requires constant attention to avoid being in situations that can disrupt your peace. When relationships hinder your growth, you must find the strength to let them go. Evaluate what you learned from your past relationships, good or bad, and allow those experiences to be used to cultivate a more fulfilling relationship in the future. Life is short. Opting out of exhausting relationships when you realize they no longer propel you toward your destiny of greatness will keep you from making empty deposits and increase your mental energy savings. Stop dating under your potential and **DUMP IT!!!**

FOUR F'S CHART

I created the self-care checklist below to keep track of how I'm caring for myself in the areas of my faith, family, fitness, and finances. I simply give myself a daily check if I have given attention to specific areas during the week. I add the total number of check marks and compare the numbers from week to week. This is just one of the many ways I check in with myself to ensure I maintain balance. Consider creating a meaningful chart that you can live by to ensure your weekly self-care needs are being met.

Four F's Chart
CHART NAME

Self-care area	Sunday	Monday	Tuesday	Wednesday	Thursday	Friday	Saturday	#
Faith	✓	✓		✓	✓	✓		5
Family	✓						✓	2
Fitness		✓		✓		✓	✓	4
Finances						✓	✓	2

Faith:
(Did daily devotion, meditate, read the Bible, prayed, journaled, attended church service, blessed someone, offered a word of encouragement, forgave offenses)

Family:
(Checked in on a loved one, spent time with family)

Fitness:
(Worked out, ate healthy)

Finances:
(**Sowed** – tithes, offerings, blessings; **Saved** – for retirement and unexpected expenses; **Spent**- paid bills, purchased something for myself, within my budget)

Sweet Reminders

If someone is not giving their best to you, they cannot bring out the best in you!

I wanted change, but I continued with my old patterns of love and was shortchanged of what I desired.

What I thought was a gain turned out to be my pain; no longer shall I remain in this unhealthy relationship that has driven me insane.

We all desire to be loved, but be careful of counterfeit love. You'll know it when you feel it; it asks much of you and gives you little in return!

Pretenders are people with words but no actions, leaving you to love their possible potential rather than their present reality!

My worth is not defined by acceptance. Experiencing your rejection has been the protection that has led me in a new direction.

YOUR BLANK CHART

*W*hat are the self-care areas you need to ensure you check in on? Name your chart and input the areas you want to weekly check in on.

Self-care area	Sunday	Monday	Tuesday	Wednesday	Thursday	Friday	Saturday	#

CHART NAME

ABOUT THE AUTHOR

*Being a voice against violence, I will be! Speaking up for
the weak, I will do! Living my life with purpose, I am!*
– Dr. Erika Lee

Erika Lee is a youth inspirational speaker and the founder
of the P. U. R. S. E. (**Partnering Under Real Situations
Every Day**) Foundation, an Atlanta-based 501(c) (3) non-
profit organization. Her organization focuses on assisting
domestic violence victims and providing education on
teen dating violence. After almost losing her life due to an
abusive relationship, she has made it her passion to help
and serve others facing the issue of abuse. She is a native of
Kankakee, Illinois and currently resides in Atlanta, Georgia.
Erika holds a bachelor's degree, a master's degree, and an
honorary doctorate for her dedication to humanity and
community service. She is a member of Delta Sigma Theta
Sorority Incorporated and attends Elizabeth Baptist Church.
Serving others is what she is called to do because she is a
God-fearing woman who has a heart for people.

Made in the USA
Columbia, SC
08 October 2021